القواعد الأربع

AL QAWAA'IDUL 'ARBA'
THE FOUR PRINCIPLES

WORK BOOK

الشيخ محمد بن عبد الوهاب

Shaykh Muhammad bin 'Abd al-Wahhaab

القواعد الأربع

The Four Fundamental Principles
Work Book

Copyright © 2010 Salafy Ink Publications

ALL RIGHTS RESERVED

No part of this Publication may be reproduced in any language, reprinted in any form or by any electronic or mechanical means, including but not limited to photocopying, recording or otherwise, without specific written consent from Salafy Ink Publications.

First Edition: Rajab 1431/June 2010

ISBN: 978-1-60585-924-8

Author: Imaam Muhammad Bin 'Abdul Wahhaab *(rahimahullah)*
Translator and compiler: Abu 'Abdis Salaam Siddiq Al Juyaanee

Published & Distributed by: Salafy Ink Publications
Visit us on the web at www.salafyink.com
Email: salafyink@gmail.com

Editing and Typesetting: **Proof 2 Print**
Email: proof2print@gmail.com

Cover Design: Usul Concept & Design (www.usuldesign.com)

Available online and in book stores.

Salafy Ink
PUBLICATIONS

Table of Contents

القواعد الأربع

لشيخ الإسلام الإمام المجدد

محمد بن عبد الوهاب

(1115–1206هـ)

. رحمه الله .

قَالَ المُؤَلِّفُ –رَحِمَهُ اللهُ–:

بِسْمِ اللهِ الرَّحْمَنِ الرَّحِيمِ

أَسْأَلُ اللهَ الكَرِيمَ ، رَبَّ العَرْشِ العَظِيمِ : أَنْ يَتَوَلَّاكَ في الدُّنْيَا وَالآخِرَةِ . وَأَنْ يَجْعَلَكَ مُبَارَكاً أَيْنَمَا كُنْتَ . وَأَنْ يَجْعَلَكَ مِمَّن إذا أُعْطِيَ شَكَرَ ، وإذا ابْتُلِيَ صَبَرَ ، وإذا أَذْنَبَ اسْتَغْفَرَ ، فَإِنَّ هَؤُلَاءِ الثَّلَاثَ عُنْوَانُ السَّعَادَةِ. اعْلَم أَرْشَدَكَ اللهُ لِطَاعَتِهِ : أَنَّ الحَنِيفِيَّةَ مِلَّةَ إبْرَاهِيمَ : أَنْ تَعْبُدَ اللهَ وَحْدَهُ مُخْلِصاً لَهُ الدِّينَ، كَمَا قَالَ تَعَالَى : ﴿ وَمَا خَلَقْتُ الجِنَّ وَالْأِنْسَ إِلَّا لِيَعْبُدُونَ ﴾

[الذريات:56]. فَإِذَا عَرَفْتَ أَنَّ اللهَ خَلَقَكَ لِعِبَادَتِهِ : فَاعْلَمْ أَنَّ العِبَادَةَ لا تُسَمَّى عِبَادَةً إلاَّ مَعَ التَّوحِيدِ ، كَمَا أَنَّ الصَّلاَةَ لا تُسَمَّى صَلاَةً إلاَّ مَعَ الطَّهَارَةِ ، فإذا دَخَلَ الشِّرْكُ في العِبَادَةِ فَسَدَتْ ، كالحَدَثِ إذَا دَخَلَ في الطَّهَارَةِ. فَإِذَا عَرَفْتَ أَنَّ الشِّرْكَ إِذَا خَالَطَ العِبَادَةَ أَفْسَدَهَا ، وَأَحْبَطَ العَمَلَ ، وصَارَ صَاحِبُهُ مِنَ الخَالِدِينَ في النَّارِ : عَرَفْتَ أَنَّ أَهَمَّ مَا عَلَيْكَ مَعْرِفَةُ ذَلِكَ ، لَعَلَّ اللهَ أَنْ يُخَلِّصَكَ مِنْ هَذِهِ الشَّبَكَةِ وهِيَ : الشِّرْكُ بالله ، الَّذِي قَالَ تَعَالَى فِيهِ : ﴿ إِنَّ اللَّهَ لا يَغْفِرُ أَنْ يُشْرَكَ بِهِ وَيَغْفِرُ مَا دُونَ ذَلِكَ لِمَنْ يَشَاءُ ﴾ [النساء: 48] وذَلِكَ بِمَعْرِفَةِ أَرْبَعِ قَوَاعِدَ ذَكَرَهَا اللهُ تَعَالى في كِتَابِهِ.

القَاعِدَةُ الأُولَى

أَنْ تَعْلَمَ أَنَّ الكُفَّارَ الذينَ قَاتَلَهُم رَسُولُ اللهِ (صلي الله عليه و سلم) مُقِرُّونَ بأَنَّ اللهَ تَعَالَى هو الخَالِقُ المُدَبِّرُ وأَنَّ ذَلِكَ لَمْ يُدْخِلْهُم في الإسْلَامِ . و الدليلُ قَوْلُهُ تَعَالَى: ﴿ قُلْ مَن يَرْزُقُكُم

مِنَ السَّمَاءِ وَالأَرْضِ أَمَّن يَمْلِكُ السَّمْعَ وَالأَبْصَارَ ، وَمَن يُخْرِجُ الْحَيَّ مِنَ الْمَيِّتِ ، وَيُخْرِجُ الْمَيِّتَ مِنَ الْحَيِّ ، وَمَن يُدَبِّرُ الأَمْرَ، فَسَيَقُولُونَ اللَّهُ فَقُلْ أَفَلاَ تَتَّقُونَ ﴾ [يونس : 31].

القَاعِدَةُ الثَّانِيةُ

أَنَّهُمْ يَقُولُونَ : مَا دَعَوْنَاهُمْ وَتَوَجَّهْنَا إِلَيهِمْ إِلاَّ لِطَلَبِ القُرْبَةِ وَالشَّفَاعَةِ .فَدَلِيلُ القُرْبَةِ قَوْلُهُ تَعَالَى: ﴿ وَالَّذِينَ اتَّخَذُوا مِنْ دُونِهِ أَوْلِيَاءَ مَا نَعْبُدُهُمْ إِلَّا لِيُقَرِّبُونَا إِلَى اللَّهِ زُلْفَى إِنَّ اللَّهَ يَحْكُمُ بَيْنَهُمْ فِي مَا هُمْ فِيهِ يَخْتَلِفُونَ إِنَّ اللَّهَ لا يَهْدِي مَنْ هُوَ كَاذِبٌ كَفَّارٌ ﴾ [الزمر:3] .وَدَلِيلُ الشَّفَاعَةِ قَوْلُهُ تَعَالَى : ﴿ وَيَعْبُدُونَ مِنْ دُونِ اللَّهِ مَا لا يَضُرُّهُمْ وَلا يَنْفَعُهُمْ وَيَقُولُونَ هَؤُلاءِ شُفَعَاؤُنَا عِنْدَ اللَّهِ ﴾ [يونس : 18] .وَالشَّفَاعَةُ شَفَاعَتَانِ : شَفَاعَةٌ مَنْفِيَّةٌ ،وَشَفَاعَةٌ مُثْبَتَةٌ. فَالشَّفَاعَةُ المَنْفِيَّةُ: مَا كَانَتْ تُطْلَبُ مِنْ غَيْرِ اللهِ فِيمَا لا يَقْدِرُ عَلَيهِ إِلَّا اللهُ. وَالدَّلِيلُ قَوْلُهُ تَعَالَى: ﴿ يَا أَيُّهَا الَّذِينَ آمَنُوا أَنْفِقُوا مِمَّا رَزَقْنَاكُمْ مِنْ قَبْلِ أَنْ يَأْتِيَ يَوْمٌ لا بَيْعٌ فِيهِ وَ لا خُلَّةٌ وَلا

شَفَاعَةٌ وَالْكَافِرُونَ هُمُ الظَّالِمُونَ﴾ [البقرة : 254]. وَالشَّفَاعَةُ المُثْبَتَةُ هِيَ: الَّتِي تُطْلَبُ مِنَ اللهِ. وَالشَّافِعُ مُكَرَّمٌ بِالشَّفَاعَةِ، وَالمَشْفُوعُ لَهُ مَنْ رَضِيَ اللهُ قَوْلَهُ وَعَمَلَهُ بعد الإذنِ، كَمَا قَالَ تَعَالَى: ﴿ مَنْ ذَا الَّذِي يَشْفَعُ عِنْدَهُ إِلَّا بِإِذْنِهِ﴾ [البقرة : 255].

القَاعِدَةُ الثَّالِثَةُ

أَنَّ النَّبِيَّ (صلي الله عليه و سلم) ظَهَرَ عَلَى أُنَاسٍ مُتَفَرِّقِينَ في عِبَادَاتِهِمْ : مِنْهُمْ مَنْ يَعْبُدُ الملائِكَةِ، و مِنْهُمْ مَنْ يَعْبُدُ الأَنبِيَاءَ والصالحينَ ، و مِنْهُمْ مَنْ يَعْبُدُ الأَشْجَارَ والأَحْجَارَ، و مِنْهُمْ مَنْ يَعْبُدُ الشَّمْسَ والقَمَرَ ، وقَاتَلَهُم رَسُولُ اللهِ (صلي الله عليه و سلم) ولم يُفَرِّقْ بَيْنَهُمْ، و الدليلُ قَوْلُهُ تَعَالَى : ﴿ وَقَاتِلُوهُمْ حَتَّى لَا تَكُونَ فِتْنَةٌ وَيَكُونَ الدِّينُ كُلُّهُ لله ﴾ [الأنفال 39]. وَدَلِيلُ الشَّمْسِ والقَمَرِ قَوْلُهُ تَعَالَى: ﴿ وَمِنْ آيَاتِهِ اللَّيْلُ وَالنَّهَارُ وَالشَّمْسُ وَالْقَمَرُ لَا تَسْجُدُوا لِلشَّمْسِ وَلَا لِلْقَمَرِ وَاسْجُدُوا لِلَّهِ الَّذِي خَلَقَهُنَّ إِنْ كُنْتُمْ إِيَّاهُ تَعْبُدُونَ ﴾ [فصلت :37] . وَدَلِيلُ الملائِكَةِ قَوْلُهُ تَعَالَى: ﴿ وَلَا يَأْمُرَكُمْ أَنْ تَتَّخِذُوا الْمَلَائِكَةَ وَالنَّبِيِّينَ أَرْبَاباً ﴾

[آل عمران : 80]. وَدَلِيلُ الأَنْبِيَاءِ قَوْلُهُ تَعَالَى: ﴿وَإِذْ قَالَ اللَّهُ يَا عِيسَى ابْنَ مَرْيَمَ أَأَنْتَ قُلْتَ لِلنَّاسِ اتَّخِذُونِي وَأُمِّيَ إِلَهَيْنِ مِنْ دُونِ اللَّهِ، قَالَ سُبْحَانَكَ مَا يَكُونُ لِي أَنْ أَقُولَ مَا لَيْسَ لِي بِحَقٍّ إِنْ كُنْتُ قُلْتُهُ فَقَدْ عَلِمْتَهُ تَعْلَمُ مَا فِي نَفْسِي وَلَا أَعْلَمُ مَا فِي نَفْسِكَ إِنَّكَ أَنْتَ عَلَّامُ الْغُيُوبِ﴾[المائدة : 116]. وَدَلِيلُ الصَّالِحِينَ قَوْلُهُ تَعَالَى: ﴿أُولَئِكَ الَّذِينَ يَدْعُونَ يَبْتَغُونَ إِلَى رَبِّهِمُ الْوَسِيلَةَ أَيُّهُمْ أَقْرَبُ وَيَرْجُونَ رَحْمَتَهُ وَيَخَافُونَ عَذَابَهُ﴾ [الإسراء:57]. وَدَلِيلُ الأَحْجَارِ وَالأَشْجَارِ قَوْلُهُ تَعَالَى: ﴿أَفَرَأَيْتُمُ اللَّاتَ وَالْعُزَّى *وَمَنَاةَ الثَّالِثَةَ الأُخْرَى﴾ [النجم:19،20]. وَحَدِيثُ أَبِي وَاقِدٍ اللَّيْثِيِّ –رَضِيَ اللَّهُ عَنْهُ– قَالَ : ((خَرَجْنَا مَعَ النَّبِي (صلي الله عليه و سلم) إِلَى حُنَيْنٍ وَنَحْنُ حُدَثَاءَ عَهْدٍ بِكُفْرٍ، وَلِلْمُشْرِكِينَ سِدْرَةٌ يَعْكُفُونَ عِنْدَهَا،وَيَنُوطُونَ بِهَا أَسْلِحَتَهُمْ يُقَالُ لَهَا : ذَاتُ أَنْوَاطٍ، فَمَرَرْنَا بِسِدْرَةٍ فَقُلْنَا : يَا رَسُولَ اللهِ اجْعَلْ لَنَا ذَاتَ أَنْوَاطٍ كَمَا لَهُمْ ذَاتُ أَنْوَاطٍ ...)) الحديث.

-8-

القَاعِدَةُ الرَّابِعَةُ

أَنَّ مُشْرِكِي زَمَانِنَا أَغْلَظُ شِرْكاً مِنْ الأُولِينَ ، لِأَنَّ الأُولِينَ يُشْرِكُونَ فِي الرَّخَاءِ وَيُخْلِصُونَ فِي الشِّدَةِ ، وَمُشْرِكُو زَمَانِنَا شِرْكُهُمْ دَائِماً فِي الرَّخَاءِ والشِّدَةِ . والدَّلِيلُ قَوْلُهُ تَعَالَى: ﴿فَإِذَا رَكِبُوا فِي الْفُلْكِ دَعَوُا اللَّهَ مُخْلِصِينَ لَهُ الدِّينَ فَلَمَّا نَجَّاهُمْ إِلَى الْبَرِّ إِذَا هُمْ يُشْرِكُونَ ﴾ [العنكبوت : 65].

تَمَّتْ وَّصَلَى اللهُ عَلَى مُحَمَّدٍ وَآلِهِ وَصَحْبِهِ وَسَلَّمَ.

<u>The Four Fundamental Principles (English Text)</u>

بِسْمِ اللهِ الرَّحْمَنِ الرَّحِيمِ

I ask Allah The Most Noble and Generous, Lord of the mighty throne, that He protects you in this world and in the hereafter; and that He makes you blessed wherever you may be. (I ask Him) to make you of those who are thankful when they are given, patient when they are tested and (quick) in seeking repentance when they sin, for verily these (three qualities) are a sign of happiness.

Know, may Allah guide you to His obedience, that Al Haneefiyyah is the way of Ibraheem (*SallAllahu 'Alaihi wa Sallam*). Verily, it is to worship Allah Alone making all of the religion sincerely for Allah, just as He The Most High says,

﴿ وَمَا خَلَقْتُ الْجِنَّ وَالْأِنْسَ إِلَّا لِيَعْبُدُونِ ﴾

"And I have not created Jinn or Mankind except to worship Me alone." [Adh Dhaariyaat: 56]

So now that you know that Allah has created you to worship Him, know that worship is neither valid nor considered worship unless it is directed to Allah alone (i.e. upon Tawheed); just as prayer is not valid without purity (i.e. Wudoo). So once Shirk enters into worship, it destroys it just as the breaking of one's Wudoo destroys the state of purity. Now that you know that Shirk -when mixed with worship- corrupts it (i.e. destroys it), invalidates action, and renders its practitioner from those who will stay in the fire forever, you will then realize that it is (imperative) that you know that the most important thing upon you is to have knowledge (and understanding of this reality), so perhaps Allah will save you from this net of associating partners with Allah. This is Shirk about which Allah says,

$$ \text{﴿ إِنَّ اللَّهَ لَا يَغْفِرُ أَنْ يُشْرَكَ بِهِ وَيَغْفِرُ مَا دُونَ ذَلِكَ لِمَنْ يَشَاءُ ﴾} $$

"Verily, Allah forgives not that partners should be set up with Him in worship, but He forgives except that (anything else) to whom He pleases, and whoever sets up partners with Allah in worship, he has indeed invented a tremendous sin." (An Nisaa: 48)

Knowing and having understanding of this can be achieved by knowing and understanding four principles which Allah The Most High mentions in His Book (i.e. The Qur'an).

<u>The First Principle</u>

The first principle is that you know that those disbelievers, whom the Messenger of Allah *(Sall Allahu 'Alaihi wa Sallam)* fought against, used to agree that Allah was The Creator, and Arranger of Affairs, but this by itself was not enough to enter them into Islaam.

The proof of this is the statement of The Most High,

﴿ قُلْ مَن يَرْزُقُكُم مِنَ السَّمَاءِ وَالأَرْضِ أَمَّن يَمْلِكُ السَّمْعَ وَالأَبْصَارَ ، وَمَن يُخْرِجُ الْحَيَّ مِنَ الْمَيِّتِ ، وَيُخْرِجُ الْمَيِّتَ مِنَ الْحَيِّ ، وَمَن يُدَبِّرُ الأَمْرَ ، فَسَيَقُولُونَ اللّهُ فَقُلْ أَفَلاَ تَتَّقُونَ ﴾

"Say (O Muhammad): "Who provides for you from the sky and from the earth? Or who owns hearing and sight? And who brings out the living from the dead and brings out the dead from the living? And who disposes the affairs?" They will say: "Allah." Say: "Will you not then be afraid of Allah's Punishment (for setting up rivals in worship with Allah)?" [Yunus: 31]

-12-

The Second Principle

Verily, the polytheists used to say, "We did not call upon the idols nor turn to them except to seek closeness and intercession (with Allah)."

The proof that they seek closeness (by way of Awliyaa) is His The Most High's statement,

$$﴿ وَالَّذِينَ اتَّخَذُوا مِنْ دُونِهِ أَوْلِيَاءَ مَا نَعْبُدُهُمْ إِلَّا لِيُقَرِّبُونَا إِلَى اللَّهِ زُلْفَى إِنَّ اللَّهَ يَحْكُمُ بَيْنَهُمْ فِي مَا هُمْ فِيهِ يَخْتَلِفُونَ إِنَّ اللَّهَ لَا يَهْدِي مَنْ هُوَ كَاذِبٌ كَفَّارٌ ﴾$$

"Surely, the religion (i.e. the worship and the obedience) is for Allah only. And those who take Awliyaa (protectors and helpers) besides Him (say): "We worship them only that they may bring us near to Allah." Verily, Allah will judge between them concerning that wherein they differ. Truly, Allah guides not him who is a liar, and a disbeliever." [Az Zumar: 3]

The proof that they seek intercession (through the Awliyaa) is His The Most High's statement,

-13-

﴿ وَيَعْبُدُونَ مِنْ دُونِ اللَّهِ مَا لَا يَضُرُّهُمْ وَلَا يَنْفَعُهُمْ وَيَقُولُونَ هَؤُلَاءِ شُفَعَاؤُنَا عِنْدَ اللَّهِ ﴾

"And they worship besides Allah things that hurt them not, nor profit them, and they say: "These are our intercessors with Allah." Say: "Do you inform Allah of that which He knows not in the heavens and on the earth?" Glorified and Exalted be He above all that which they associate as partners with Him!" [Yunus: 18]

Shafaa'ah (Intercession) is of two types:

1. **Shafaa'ah Manfiyyah** (The Prohibited Intercession)
2. **Shafaa'ah Muthbatah** (The Affirmed Intercession)

Shafaa'ah Manfiyyah is that which is sought from other than Allah, in that which none has the ability to do except Allah, the proof is His The Most High's statement,

﴿ يَا أَيُّهَا الَّذِينَ آمَنُوا أَنْفِقُوا مِمَّا رَزَقْنَاكُمْ مِنْ قَبْلِ أَنْ يَأْتِيَ يَوْمٌ لَا بَيْعٌ فِيهِ وَلَا خُلَّةٌ وَلَا شَفَاعَةٌ وَالْكَافِرُونَ هُمُ الظَّالِمُونَ ﴾

"O you who believe! Spend of that with which We have provided for you, before a Day comes when there will be no bargaining, nor friendship, nor intercession. And it is the disbelievers who are the wrong-doers." [Al Baqarah: 254]

Shafaa'ah Muthbatah is that which is sought from Allah, the one who intercedes is honored with the intercession while the one being interceded for is one whose statements and actions Allah is pleased with, (thus intercession is given to that one) after the permission of Allah is granted, just as Allah says,

$$﴿ مَنْ ذَا الَّذِي يَشْفَعُ عِنْدَهُ إِلَّا بِإِذْنِهِ ﴾$$

"Who is he that can intercede with Him except with His Permission?" [Al Baqarah: 255]

The Third Principle

The Prophet *(Sall-Allahu 'Alaihi wa Sallam)* encountered a people who were different with regards to that which they worshipped. From them were those who used to worship the Angels, others who used to worship the Prophets and the Righteous, while others used to worship trees and stones, and others used to worship the sun and the moon.

The Messenger of Allah *(Sall-Allahu 'Alaihi wa Sallam)* used to fight against all of them and he did not make any distinction between them. The proof of this is Allah's The Most High's statement,

﴿ وَقَاتِلُوهُمْ حَتَّىٰ لَا تَكُونَ فِتْنَةٌ وَيَكُونَ الدِّينُ كُلُّهُ لله ﴾

"And fight them until there is no more Fitnah (disbelief and polytheism: i.e. worshipping others besides Allah) and the religion (worship) will all be for Allah Alone."
[Al Anfal: 39]

The proof that the sun and the moon are worshipped is The Most High's statement,

﴿ وَمِنْ آيَاتِهِ اللَّيْلُ وَالنَّهَارُ وَالشَّمْسُ وَالْقَمَرُ لَا تَسْجُدُوا لِلشَّمْسِ وَلَا لِلْقَمَرِ وَاسْجُدُوا لِلَّهِ الَّذِي خَلَقَهُنَّ إِنْ كُنْتُمْ إِيَّاهُ تَعْبُدُونَ ﴾

"And from among His Signs are the night and the day, and the sun and the moon. Prostrate neither to the sun nor to the moon, but prostrate to Allah Who created them, if you (really) worship Him." [Al Fussilat: 37]

The proof that the Angels are worshipped is The Most High's statement,

﴿ وَلَا يَأْمُرَكُمْ أَنْ تَتَّخِذُوا الْمَلَائِكَةَ وَالنَّبِيِّينَ أَرْبَاباً ﴾

"Nor would he order you to take Angels and Prophets for lords (gods). [Aali 'Imraan: 80]

The proof that the Prophets are worshipped is The Most High's statement,

﴿ وَإِذْ قَالَ اللَّهُ يَا عِيسَى ابْنَ مَرْيَمَ أَأَنْتَ قُلْتَ لِلنَّاسِ اتَّخِذُونِي وَأُمِّيَ إِلَهَيْنِ مِنْ دُونِ اللَّهِ، قَالَ سُبْحَانَكَ مَا يَكُونُ لِي أَنْ أَقُولَ مَا لَيْسَ لِي بِحَقٍّ إِنْ كُنْتُ قُلْتُهُ فَقَدْ عَلِمْتَهُ تَعْلَمُ مَا فِي نَفْسِي وَلَا أَعْلَمُ مَا فِي نَفْسِكَ إِنَّكَ أَنْتَ عَلَّامُ الْغُيُوبِ ﴾

"And (remember) when Allah will say (on the Day of Resurrection): "O 'Iesa (Jesus), son of Maryam (Mary)! Did you say unto men: 'Worship me and my mother as two gods besides Allah?' "He will say: "Glory be to You! It was not for me to say what I had no right (to say). Had I said such a thing, You would surely have known it. You know what is in my inner self though I do not know what is in Yours, truly, You, only You, are the All Knower of all that is hidden and unseen." [Al Ma'idah: 116]

The proof that the righteous are worshipped is The Most High's statement,

﴿ أُولَٰئِكَ الَّذِينَ يَدْعُونَ يَبْتَغُونَ إِلَىٰ رَبِّهِمُ الْوَسِيلَةَ أَيُّهُمْ أَقْرَبُ وَيَرْجُونَ رَحْمَتَهُ وَيَخَافُونَ عَذَابَهُ ﴾

"Those whom they call upon [like 'Iesa (Jesus) son of Maryam (Mary), 'Uzair (Ezra), Angels, etc.] desire (for themselves) means of access to their Lord (Allah), as to which of them should be the nearest and they ['Iesa (Jesus), 'Uzair (Ezra), Angels, etc.] hope for His Mercy and fear His Torment." [Al Israa: 57]

The proof that stones and trees are worshipped is The Most High's statement,

﴿ أَفَرَأَيْتُمُ اللَّاتَ وَالْعُزَّىٰ (19) وَمَنَاةَ الثَّالِثَةَ الْأُخْرَىٰ (20) ﴾

"Have you then considered Al-Laat, and Al-'Uzza (two idols of the pagan Arabs) and Manaat (another idol of the pagan Arabs) the other third?" [An Najm: 19-20]

And the Hadeeth of Abee Waaqid Al Laithee,

((خَرَجْنَا مَعَ النَّبِي (صلي الله عليه و سلم) إلى حُنَيْنٍ وَنَحْنُ حُدَثَاءَ عَهْدٍ بِكُفْرٍ، وَلِلْمُشْرِكِينَ سِدْرَةٌ يَعْكُفُونَ عِنْدَهَا، وَيَنُوطُونَ

بِهَا أَسْلِحَتَهُم يُقَالُ لَهَا : ذَاتُ أَنْوَاطٍ، فَمَرَرْنَا بِسِدْرَةٍ فَقُلْنَا : يَا

رَسُولَ اللهِ اجْعَلْ لَنَا ذَاتَ أَنْوَاطٍ كَمَا لَهُمْ ذَاتُ أَنْوَاطٍ ...))

"We departed with the Prophet to Hunain and we had recently left disbelief (i.e. we were new Muslims). The polytheists had a tree which they used to devote themselves to and hang their weapons upon, which was called Thaatu Anwaat. We passed by a tree and said, "O Messenger of Allah make for us a Thaatu Anwaat just as they have a Thaatu Anwaat... (until the end of the Hadeeth)."

The Fourth Principle

Verily, the polytheists of our time are more extreme in their polytheism than the polytheists of old. This is because the polytheists of old would only commit polytheistic acts during times of ease, but they purely (called upon Allah during) times of hardship; whereas the polytheists of our time perpetually commit polytheistic acts, (both) during times of ease and hardship.

The proof (that the polytheists of old would only committed polytheistic acts during times of ease but purely (calling upon Allah during) times of hardship is His, The Most High's statement,

$$\text{﴿ فَإِذَا رَكِبُوا فِي الْفُلْكِ دَعَوُا اللَّهَ مُخْلِصِينَ لَهُ الدِّينَ فَلَمَّا نَجَّاهُمْ إِلَى الْبَرِّ إِذَا هُمْ يُشْرِكُونَ ﴾}$$

"And when they embark on a ship, they invoke Allah, making their Faith pure for Him only, but when He brings them safely to land, behold, they give a share of their worship to others." [Al 'Ankabut: 65]

The Four Fundamental Principles Work Book

بِسْمِ اللهِ الرَّحْمَنِ الرَّحِيمِ

I ask Allah The Most Noble and Generous, Lord of the mighty throne, that He protects you in this world and in the hereafter; and that He makes you blessed wherever you may be. (I ask Him) to make you of those who are thankful when they are given, patient when they are tested and (quick) in seeking repentance when they sin, for verily these (three qualities) are a sign of happiness.

Know, may Allah guide you to His obedience, that Al Haneefiyyah is the way of Ibraheem *(Sall-Allahu 'Alaihi wa Sallam)*. Verily, it is to worship Allah Alone making all of the religion sincerely for Allah, just as He The Most High says,

﴿ وَمَا خَلَقْتُ الْجِنَّ وَالْإِنْسَ إِلَّا لِيَعْبُدُونِ ﴾

"And I have not created Jinn or Mankind except to worship Me alone." [Adh Dhaariyaat: 56]

So now that you know that Allah has created you to worship Him, know that worship is neither valid nor considered worship unless it is directed to Allah alone (i.e. upon Tawheed); just as prayer is not valid without purity (i.e. Wudoo). So once Shirk enters into worship, it destroys it just as the breaking of one's Wudoo destroys the state of purity. Now that you know that Shirk -when mixed with worship- corrupts it (i.e. destroys it), invalidates action, and renders its practitioner from those who will stay in the fire forever, you will then realize that it is (imperative) that you know that the most important thing upon you is to have knowledge (and understanding of this reality), so perhaps Allah will save you from this net of associating partners with Allah. This is Shirk about which Allah says,

$$﴿ إِنَّ اللَّهَ لَا يَغْفِرُ أَنْ يُشْرَكَ بِهِ وَيَغْفِرُ مَا دُونَ ذَلِكَ لِمَنْ يَشَاءُ ﴾$$

"Verily, Allah forgives not that partners should be set up with Him in worship, but He forgives except that (anything else) to whom He pleases, and whoever sets up partners with Allah in worship, he has indeed invented a tremendous sin." (An Nisaa: 48)

Knowing and having understanding of this can be achieved by knowing and understanding four principles which Allah The Most High mentions in His Book (i.e. The Qur'an).

-23-

<u>Review Questions on the Shaikh's Introduction</u>

1. What are the three signs of happiness?

_____

_____

_____

_____

2. What is Al Haneefiyyah?

_____

_____

_____

_____

_____

_____

_____

3. What is the proof the Shaikh (*rahimahullah*) brings for the previous answer?

_____

_____

_____

_____

4. Why did Allah (*Azza wa Jal*) create you?

_____

_____

_____

_____

5. When is worship valid and truly considered worship?

_____

_____

6. Write out the example the Shaikh *(rahimahullah)* used to illustrate the answer of the previous question.

_____

_____

_____

_____

_____

7. What affect does shirk have on worship, and what does it
   do to it when it enters it?

_____

_____

_____

_____

_____

_____

_____

8. What does Allah say about shirk?

The First Principle

The first principle is that you know that those disbelievers, whom the Messenger of Allah (*Sall-Allahu 'Alaihi wa Sallam*) fought against, used to agree that Allah was The Creator, and Arranger of Affairs, but this by itself was not enough to enter them into Islaam.

The proof of this is the statement of The Most High,

$$\text{﴿ قُلْ مَن يَرْزُقُكُم مِنَ السَّمَآءِ وَالأَرْضِ أَمَّن يَمْلِكُ السَّمْعَ وَالأَبْصَارَ ، وَمَن يُخْرِجُ الْحَيّ مِنَ الْمَيِّتِ ، وَيُخْرِجُ الْمَيّتَ مِنَ الْحَيّ وَمَن يُدَبِّرُ الأَمْرَ ، فَسَيَقُولُونَ اللَّهُ فَقُلْ أَفَلاَ تَتَّقُونَ ﴾}$$

"Say (O Muhammad): "Who provides for you from the sky and from the earth? Or who owns hearing and sight? And who brings out the living from the dead and brings out the dead from the living? And who disposes the affairs?" They will say: "Allah." Say: "Will you not then be afraid of Allah's Punishment (for setting up rivals in worship with Allah)?" [Yunus: 31]

<u>Review Questions on The First Principle</u>

1. What do the disbelievers whom the Messenger of Allah (*SallAllaahu Alaihi wa Sallam*) fought against agree with?

_____

_____

_____

_____

2. Does their agreement with, and belief in this affair make them Muslims?

_____

_____

_____

3. What is the proof to the previous answer?

_____

_____

_____

_____

<u>The Second Principle</u>

Verily, the polytheists used to say, "We did not call upon the idols nor turn to them except to seek closeness and intercession (with Allah)."

The proof that they seek closeness (by way of Awliyaa) is His The Most High's statement,

$$﴿ وَالَّذِينَ اتَّخَذُوا مِنْ دُونِهِ أَوْلِيَاءَ مَا نَعْبُدُهُمْ إِلَّا لِيُقَرِّبُونَا إِلَى اللَّهِ زُلْفَى إِنَّ اللَّهَ يَحْكُمُ بَيْنَهُمْ فِي مَا هُمْ فِيهِ يَخْتَلِفُونَ إِنَّ اللَّهَ لَا يَهْدِي مَنْ هُوَ كَاذِبٌ كَفَّارٌ ﴾$$

"Surely, the religion (i.e. the worship and the obedience) is for Allah only. And those who take Awliyaa (protectors and helpers) besides Him (say): "We worship them only that they may bring us near to Allah." Verily, Allah will judge between them concerning that wherein they differ. Truly, Allah guides not him who is a liar, and a disbeliever." [Az Zumar: 3]

The proof that they seek intercession (through the Awliyaa) is His The Most High's statement,

﴿ وَيَعْبُدُونَ مِنْ دُونِ اللَّهِ مَا لَا يَضُرُّهُمْ وَلَا يَنْفَعُهُمْ وَيَقُولُونَ هَؤُلَاءِ شُفَعَاؤُنَا عِنْدَ اللَّهِ ﴾

"And they worship besides Allah things that hurt them not, nor profit them, and they say: "These are our intercessors with Allah." Say: "Do you inform Allah of that which He knows not in the heavens and on the earth?" Glorified and Exalted be He above all that which they associate as partners with Him!" [Yunus: 18]

Shafaa'ah (Intercession) is of two types:

1. **Shafaa'ah Manfiyyah** (The Prohibited Intercession)
2. **Shafaa'ah Muthbatah** (The Affirmed Intercession)

Shafaa'ah Manfiyyah is that which is sought from other than Allah, in that which none has the ability to do except Allah, the proof is His The Most High's statement,

﴿ يَا أَيُّهَا الَّذِينَ آمَنُوا أَنْفِقُوا مِمَّا رَزَقْنَاكُمْ مِنْ قَبْلِ أَنْ يَأْتِيَ يَوْمٌ لَا بَيْعٌ فِيهِ وَلَا خُلَّةٌ وَلَا شَفَاعَةٌ وَالْكَافِرُونَ هُمُ الظَّالِمُونَ ﴾

"O you who believe! Spend of that with which We have provided for you, before a Day comes when there will be no bargaining, nor friendship, nor intercession. And it is the disbelievers who are the wrong-doers." [Al Baqarah: 254]

Shafaa'ah Muthbatah is that which is sought from Allah, the one who intercedes is honored with the intercession while the one being interceded for is one whose statements and actions Allah is pleased with, (thus intercession is given to that one) after the permission of Allah is granted, just as Allah says,

$$﴿ مَنْ ذَا الَّذِي يَشْفَعُ عِنْدَهُ إِلَّا بِإِذْنِهِ ﴾$$

"Who is he that can intercede with Him except with His Permission?" [Al Baqarah: 255]

❀ ❀ ❀

<u>Review Questions on The Second Principle</u>

1. What was the reason given by the polytheists for making shirk?

_____

_____

_____

_____

2. What is the proof for the previous answer?

_____

_____

_____

_____

_____

_____

3. How many types of intercession are there?

4. State the types of intersession with their definitions and proofs.

The Third Principle

The Prophet (Sall-Allahu 'Alaihi wa Sallam) encountered a people who were different with regards to that which they worshipped. From them were those who used to worship the Angels, others who used to worship the Prophets and the Righteous, while others used to worship trees and stones, and others used to worship the sun and the moon.

The Messenger of Allah (Sall-Allahu 'Alaihi wa Sallam) used to fight against all of them and he did not make any distinction between them. The proof of this is Allah's The Most High's statement,

$$\text{﴿ وَقَاتِلُوهُمْ حَتَّى لاَ تَكُونَ فِتْنَةٌ وَيَكُونَ الدِّينُ كُلُّهُ لله ﴾}$$

"And fight them until there is no more Fitnah (disbelief and polytheism: i.e. worshipping others besides Allah) and the religion (worship) will all be for Allah Alone."
[Al Anfal: 39]

The proof that the sun and the moon are worshipped is The Most High's statement,

﴿ وَمِنْ آيَاتِهِ اللَّيْلُ وَالنَّهَارُ وَالشَّمْسُ وَالْقَمَرُ لَا تَسْجُدُوا لِلشَّمْسِ وَلَا لِلْقَمَرِ وَاسْجُدُوا لِلَّهِ الَّذِي خَلَقَهُنَّ إِنْ كُنْتُمْ إِيَّاهُ تَعْبُدُونَ ﴾

"And from among His Signs are the night and the day, and the sun and the moon. Prostrate neither to the sun nor to the moon, but prostrate to Allah Who created them, if you (really) worship Him." [Al Fussilat: 37]

The proof that the Angels are worshipped is The Most High's statement,

﴿ وَلَا يَأْمُرَكُمْ أَنْ تَتَّخِذُوا الْمَلَائِكَةَ وَالنَّبِيِّينَ أَرْبَاباً ﴾

"Nor would he order you to take Angels and Prophets for lords (gods). [Aali 'Imraan: 80]

The proof that the Prophets are worshipped is The Most High's statement,

﴿ وَإِذْ قَالَ اللَّهُ يَا عِيسَى ابْنَ مَرْيَمَ أَأَنْتَ قُلْتَ لِلنَّاسِ اتَّخِذُونِي وَأُمِّيَ إِلَهَيْنِ مِنْ دُونِ اللَّهِ، قَالَ سُبْحَانَكَ مَا يَكُونُ لِي أَنْ أَقُولَ مَا لَيْسَ لِي بِحَقٍّ إِنْ كُنْتُ قُلْتُهُ فَقَدْ عَلِمْتَهُ تَعْلَمُ مَا فِي نَفْسِي وَلَا أَعْلَمُ مَا فِي نَفْسِكَ إِنَّكَ أَنْتَ عَلَّامُ الْغُيُوبِ ﴾

"And (remember) when Allah will say (on the Day of Resurrection): "O 'Iesa (Jesus), son of Maryam (Mary)! Did you say unto men: 'Worship me and my mother as two gods besides Allah?' "He will say: "Glory be to You! It was not for me to say what I had no right (to say). Had I said such a thing, You would surely have known it. You know what is in my inner self though I do not know what is in Yours, truly, You, only You, are the All Knower of all that is hidden and unseen." [Al Ma'idah: 116]

The proof that the righteous are worshipped is The Most High's statement,

$$ \text{﴿ أُولَئِكَ الَّذِينَ يَدْعُونَ يَبْتَغُونَ إِلَى رَبِّهِمُ الْوَسِيلَةَ أَيُّهُمْ أَقْرَبُ وَيَرْجُونَ رَحْمَتَهُ وَيَخَافُونَ عَذَابَهُ ﴾} $$

"Those whom they call upon [like 'Iesa (Jesus) son of Maryam (Mary), 'Uzair (Ezra), Angels, etc.] desire (for themselves) means of access to their Lord (Allah), as to which of them should be the nearest and they ['Iesa (Jesus), 'Uzair (Ezra), Angels, etc.] hope for His Mercy and fear His Torment." [Al Israa: 57]

The proof that stones and trees are worshipped is The Most High's statement,

$$ ﴿ أَفَرَأَيْتُمُ اللَّاتَ وَالْعُزَّى (19) وَمَنَاةَ الثَّالِثَةَ الْأُخْرَى (20) ﴾ $$

"Have you then considered Al-Laat, and Al-'Uzza (two idols of the pagan Arabs) and Manaat (another idol of the pagan Arabs) the other third?" [An Najm: 19-20]

And the Hadeeth of Abee Waaqid Al Laithee,

((خَرَجْنَا مَعَ النَّبِي (صلي الله عليه و سلم) إلى حُنَيْنٍ وَنَحْنُ حُدَثَاءَ عَهْدٍ بِكُفْرٍ، وَلِلْمُشْرِكِينَ سِدْرَةٌ يَعْكُفُونَ عِنْدَهَا، وَيَنُوطُونَ بِهَا أَسْلِحَتَهُمْ يُقَالُ لَهَا : ذَاتُ أَنْوَاطٍ، فَمَرَرْنَا بِسِدْرَةٍ فَقُلْنَا : يَا رَسُولَ اللهِ اجْعَلْ لَنَا ذَاتَ أَنْوَاطٍ كَمَا لَهُمْ ذَاتُ أَنْوَاطٍ ...))

"We departed with the Prophet to Hunain and we had recently left disbelief (i.e. we were new Muslims). The polytheists had a tree which they used to devote themselves to and hang their weapons upon, which was called Thaatu Anwaat. We passed by a tree and said, "O Messenger of Allah make for us a Thaatu Anwaat just as they have a Thaatu Anwaat... (until the end of the Hadeeth)."

<u>Review Questions on The Third Principle</u>

1. Finish the following paragraph,

   "The Prophet encountered a people who were different with regards to that which they worshipped..."

   _____

   _____

   _____

   _____

   _____

   _____

   _____

2. What is the proof that the sun and the moon are worshipped?

   _____

   _____

   _____

_____

_____

_____

_____

3. What is the proof that the Angels are worshipped?

_____

_____

_____

_____

4. What is the proof that the Prophets are worshipped?

_____

_____

_____

_____

_____

_____

_____

_____

5. What is the proof that the righteous are worshipped?

_____

_____

_____

_____

6. What is the proof that stones and trees are worshipped?

_____

_____

_____

_____

_____

<u>The Fourth Principle</u>

Verily, the polytheists of our time are more extreme in their polytheism than the polytheists of old. This is because the polytheists of old would only commit polytheistic acts during times of ease, but they purely (called upon Allah during) times of hardship; whereas the polytheists of our time perpetually commit polytheistic acts, (both) during times of ease and hardship.

The proof (that the polytheists of old would only committed polytheistic acts during times of ease but purely (called upon Allah during) times of hardship is His, The Most High's statement,

$$\text{﴿ فَإِذَا رَكِبُوا فِي الْفُلْكِ دَعَوُا اللَّهَ مُخْلِصِينَ لَهُ الدِّينَ فَلَمَّا نَجَّاهُمْ إِلَى الْبَرِّ إِذَا هُمْ يُشْرِكُونَ ﴾}$$

"And when they embark on a ship, they invoke Allah, making their Faith pure for Him only, but when He brings them safely to land, behold, they give a share of their worship to others." [Al 'Ankabut: 65]

<u>Review Questions on The Fourth Principle</u>

1. Why are the polytheists of our time more extreme in their polytheism than the polytheists of old?

_____

_____

_____

_____

_____

2. What is the proof (that the polytheists of old would only committed polytheistic acts during times of ease but purely (called upon Allah during) times of hardship?

_____

_____

_____

_____

Test Prep

1. What are the three signs of happiness?

A. To be thankful when given, patient when tested and (quick) in seeking repentance.

2. What is Al Haneefiyyah?

A. Al Haneefiyyah is the way of Ibraheem *(Sall-Allahu Alaihi wa Sallam)* ; Verily, it is to worship Allah alone making all of the religion sincerely for Allah.

3. What is the proof the Shaikh *(rahimahullah)* brings for the previous answer?

A.

$$﴿ وَمَا خَلَقْتُ الْجِنَّ وَالْأِنْسَ إِلَّا لِيَعْبُدُونِ ﴾$$

"And I have not created Jinn or Mankind except to worship Me alone" [Adh Dhaariyaat: 56]

4. Why did Allah *(Azza wa Jal)* create you?

A. Allah created me to worship Him alone.

5. When is worship valid and truly considered worship?

A. Worship is only valid and considered worship when it is directed to Allah alone (i.e. upon Tawheed).

6. Write out the example the Shaikh (*rahimahullah*) used to illustrate the answer of the previous question.

A. Prayer is not valid without purity (i.e. Wudoo). So once Shirk enters into worship it destroys it just as the breaking of one's Wudoo destroys the state of purity.

7. What affect does shirk have on worship, and what does it do to it when it enters it?

A. Once Shirk enters into worship it destroys it.

8. What does Allah say about shirk?

A.

$$﴿ إِنَّ اللَّهَ لَا يَغْفِرُ أَنْ يُشْرَكَ بِهِ وَيَغْفِرُ مَا دُونَ ذَلِكَ لِمَنْ يَشَاءُ ﴾$$

"Verily, Allah forgives not that partners should be set up with him in worship, but He forgives except that (anything else) to whom He pleases, and whoever sets up partners with Allah in worship, he has indeed invented a tremendous sin." (An Nisaa: 48)

9. What do the disbelievers whom the Messenger of Allah (*SallAllahu Alaihi wa Sallam*) fought against agree with?

A. They used to agree that Allah was The Creator, and Arranger of Affairs.

10. Does their agreement with, and belief in this affair make them Muslims?

A. NO!

11. What is the proof to the previous answer?

A.

﴿ قُلْ مَن يَرْزُقُكُم مِنَ السَّمَاءِ وَالأَرْضِ أَمَّن يَمْلِكُ السَّمْعَ وَالأَبْصَارَ ، وَمَن يُخْرِجُ الْحَيَّ مِنَ الْمَيِّتِ ، وَيُخْرِجُ الْمَيِّتَ مِنَ الْحَيِّ وَمَن يُدَبِّرُ الأَمْرَ ، فَسَيَقُولُونَ اللّهُ فَقُلْ أَفَلاَ تَتَّقُونَ ﴾

Say (O Muhammad): "Who provides for you from the sky and from the earth? Or who owns hearing and sight? And who brings out the living from the dead and brings out the dead from the living? And who disposes the affairs?" They will say: "Allah." Say: "Will you not then be afraid of Allah's Punishment (for setting up rivals in worship with Allah)?" [Yunus: 31]

12. What was the reason given by the polytheists give for making shirk?

A. They say, "We did not call upon the idols nor turn to them except to seek closeness and intercession (with Allah)."

13. What is the proof for the previous answer?

A.

$$﴿ وَالَّذِينَ اتَّخَذُوا مِنْ دُونِهِ أَوْلِيَاءَ مَا نَعْبُدُهُمْ إِلَّا لِيُقَرِّبُونَا إِلَى اللَّهِ زُلْفَى إِنَّ اللَّهَ يَحْكُمُ بَيْنَهُمْ فِي مَا هُمْ فِيهِ يَخْتَلِفُونَ إِنَّ اللَّهَ لَا يَهْدِي مَنْ هُوَ كَاذِبٌ كَفَّارٌ ﴾$$

"Surely, the religion (i.e. the worship and the obedience) is for Allah only. And those who take Awliyaa (protectors and helpers) besides Him (say): "We worship them only that they may bring us near to Allah." Verily, Allah will judge between them concerning that wherein they differ. Truly, Allah guides not him who is a liar, and a disbeliever."
[Az Zumar: 3]

14. How many types of intercession are there?

A. There are two types of intercession.

15. State the types of intersession with their definitions and proofs.

A. Shafaa'ah Manfiyyah is that which is sought from other than Allah, in that which none has the ability to do except Allah, the proof is His, The Most High's statement,

﴿ يَا أَيُّهَا الَّذِينَ آمَنُوا أَنْفِقُوا مِمَّا رَزَقْنَاكُمْ مِنْ قَبْلِ أَنْ يَأْتِيَ يَوْمٌ لَا بَيْعٌ فِيهِ وَلَا خُلَّةٌ وَلَا شَفَاعَةٌ وَالْكَافِرُونَ هُمُ الظَّالِمُونَ ﴾

"O you who believe! Spend of that with which We have provided for you, before a Day comes when there will be no bargaining, nor friendship, nor intercession. And it is the disbelievers who are the wrong-doers." [Al Baqarah: 254]

Shafaa'ah Muthbatah is that which is sought from Allah, the one who intercedes is honored with the intercession while the one being interceded for is one whom Allah is pleased with their statements and actions, (thus intercession is give to that one) after the permission of Allah is granted, just as Allah says,

﴿ مَنْ ذَا الَّذِي يَشْفَعُ عِنْدَهُ إِلَّا بِإِذْنِهِ ﴾

"Who is he that can intercede with Him except with His Permission?" [Al Baqarah: 255]

16. Finish the following paragraph, "The Prophet encountered a people who were different with regards to that which they worshipped…"

A. The Prophet (*Sall Allahu 'Alaihi wa Sallam*) encountered a people who were different with regards to that which they worshipped. From them were those who used to worship the Angels, others who used to worship the Prophets and the Righteous, while others used to worship trees and stones, and others used to worship the sun and moon. The Messenger of Allah use to fight against all and he did not make any distinction between them.

The proof of this is Allah's The Most High's statement,

$$﴿ وَقَاتِلُوهُمْ حَتَّى لَا تَكُونَ فِتْنَةٌ وَيَكُونَ الدِّينُ كُلُّهُ لله ﴾$$

"And fight them until there is no more Fitnah (disbelief and polytheism: i.e. worshipping others besides Allah) and the religion (worship) will all be for Allah Alone." [Al Anfal: 39]

17. What is the proof that the sun and the moon are worshipped?

A.

$$﴿ وَمِنْ آيَاتِهِ اللَّيْلُ وَالنَّهَارُ وَالشَّمْسُ وَالْقَمَرُ لا تَسْجُدُوا لِلشَّمْسِ$$
$$وَلا لِلْقَمَرِ وَاسْجُدُوا لِلَّهِ الَّذِي خَلَقَهُنَّ إِنْ كُنْتُمْ إِيَّاهُ تَعْبُدُونَ ﴾$$

"And from among His Signs are the night and the day, and the sun and the moon. Prostrate not to the sun nor to the moon, but prostrate to Allah Who created them, if you (really) worship Him." [Al Fussilat: 37]

18. What is the proof that the Angels are worshipped?

A.

﴿ وَلَا يَأْمُرَكُمْ أَنْ تَتَّخِذُوا الْمَلَائِكَةَ وَالنَّبِيِّينَ أَرْبَاباً ﴾

"Nor would he order you to take angels and Prophets for lords (gods). Would he order you to disbelieve after you have submitted to Allah's Will?" [Aali Imraan: 80]

19. What is the proof that the Prophets are worshipped?

A.

﴿ وَإِذْ قَالَ اللَّهُ يَا عِيسَى ابْنَ مَرْيَمَ أَأَنْتَ قُلْتَ لِلنَّاسِ اتَّخِذُونِي وَأُمِّيَ إِلَهَيْنِ مِنْ دُونِ اللَّهِ، قَالَ سُبْحَانَكَ مَا يَكُونُ لِي أَنْ أَقُولَ مَا لَيْسَ لِي بِحَقٍّ إِنْ كُنْتُ قُلْتُهُ فَقَدْ عَلِمْتَهُ تَعْلَمُ مَا فِي نَفْسِي وَلَا أَعْلَمُ مَا فِي نَفْسِكَ إِنَّكَ أَنْتَ عَلَّامُ الْغُيُوبِ ﴾

"And (remember) when Allah will say (on the Day of Resurrection): "O 'Iesa (Jesus), son of Maryam (Mary)! Did you say unto men: 'Worship me and my mother as two gods besides Allah?' " He will say: "Glory be to You! It was not for me to say what I had no right (to say). Had I said such a thing, You would surely have known it. You know what is in my inner self though I do not know what is in Yours, truly, You, only You, are the All Knower of all that is hidden and unseen." [Al Ma'idah: 116]

20. What is the proof that the righteous are worshipped?

A.

﴿ أُولَٰئِكَ الَّذِينَ يَدْعُونَ يَبْتَغُونَ إِلَىٰ رَبِّهِمُ الْوَسِيلَةَ أَيُّهُمْ أَقْرَبُ وَيَرْجُونَ رَحْمَتَهُ وَيَخَافُونَ عَذَابَهُ ﴾

"Those whom they call upon [like 'Iesa (Jesus) son of Maryam (Mary), 'Uzair (Ezra), angel, etc.] desire (for themselves) means of access to their Lord (Allâh), as to which of them should be the nearest and they ['Iesa (Jesus), 'Uzair (Ezra), angels, etc.] hope for His Mercy and fear His Torment." [Al Israa: 57]

21. What is the proof that stones and trees are worshipped?

A.

﴿ أَفَرَأَيْتُمُ اللَّاتَ وَالْعُزَّى (19) وَمَنَاةَ الثَّالِثَةَ الْأُخْرَى (20)﴾

"Have you then considered Al-Laat, and Al-'Uzza (two idols of the pagan Arabs) And Manaat (another idol of thepagan Arabs), the other third?" [An Najm: 19-20]

And the Hadeeth of Abee Waaqid Al Laithee,

((خَرَجْنَا مَعَ النَّبِي (صلي الله عليه و سلم) إلى حُنَيْنٍ وَنَحْنُ حُدَثَاءَ عَهْدٍ بِكُفْرٍ، وَلِلْمُشْرِكِينَ سِدْرَةٌ يَعْكُفُونَ عِنْدَهَا،وَيُنُوطُونَ بِهَا أَسْلِحَتَهُم يُقَالُ لَهَا : ذَاتُ أَنْوَاطٍ، فَمَرَرْنَا بِسِدْرَةٍ فَقُلْنَا : يَا رَسُولَ اللهِ اجْعَلْ لَنَا ذَاتَ أَنْوَاطٍ كَمَا لَهُمْ ذَاتُ أَنْوَاطٍ ...))

We departed with the Prophet to Hunain and we had recently left disbelief (i.e. we were new Muslims). The polytheists had a tree which they used to devote themselves to and hang their weapons upon, which was called Thaatu Anwaat. We passed by a tree and said, "O Messenger of Allah make for us a Thaatu Anwaat just as they have a Thaatu Anwaat... (until the end of the Hadeeth).

22. Why are the polytheists of our time more extreme in their polytheism than the polytheists of old?

A. The polytheists of our time are more extreme in their polytheism than the polytheists of old because the polytheists of old would only commit polytheistic acts during times of ease but purely (called upon Allah during) times of hardship; whereas the polytheists of our time perpetually commit polytheistic acts, (both) during times of ease and hardship.

23. What is that the proof (that the polytheists of old would only commit polytheistic acts during times of ease but purely (called upon Allah during) times of hardship?

A.

$$ \text{﴾ فَإِذَا رَكِبُوا فِي الْفُلْكِ دَعَوُا اللَّهَ مُخْلِصِينَ لَهُ الدِّينَ فَلَمَّا نَجَّاهُمْ إِلَى الْبَرِّ إِذَا هُمْ يُشْرِكُونَ ﴿} $$

"And when they embark on a ship, they invoke Allah, making their Faith pure for Him only, but when He brings them safely to land, behold, they give a share of their worship to others." [Al 'Ankabut: 65]